OLE MISS
REBELS

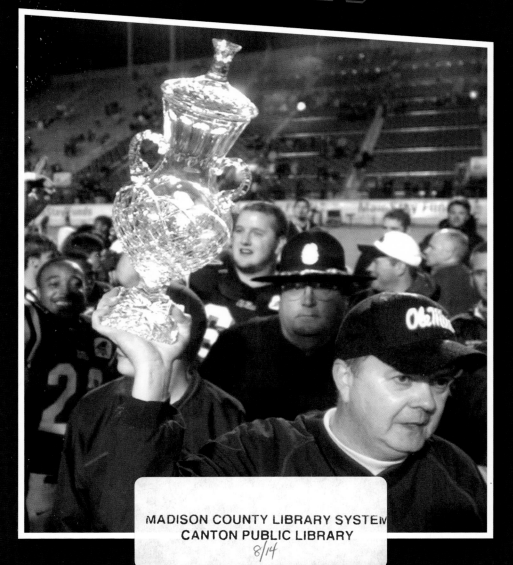

BY MARTY GITLIN

Published by ABDO Publishing Company, PO Box 398166, Minneapolis, MN 55439. Copyright © 2013 by Abdo Consulting Group, Inc. International copyrights reserved in all countries. No part of this book may be reproduced in any form without written permission from the publisher. SportsZone™ is a trademark and logo of ABDO Publishing Company.

Printed in the United States of America,
North Mankato, Minnesota
112012
012013

 THIS BOOK CONTAINS AT LEAST 10% RECYCLED MATERIALS.

Editor: Chrös McDougall
Series Designer: Craig Hinton

Photo Credits: Oxford Eagle, Bruce Newman/AP Images, cover; Rogelio Solis/AP Images, title, 9, 34, 43 (bottom, right), 44; Tony Gutierrez/AP Images, 4, 11, 43 (bottom, left); Brian Bahr/Getty Images, 7; University of Mississippi/Getty Images, 12, 18, 25, 28, 31, 42 (top, left and right); Pictorial Parade/Getty Images, 17; AP Images, 21; Mississippi/Collegiate Images/Getty Images, 23, 43, (top); Art Shay/Sports Illustrated/Getty Images, 26, 42 (bottom); William Maslin/AP Images, 32; Kevin Bain/AP Images, 37; Joe Murphy/WireImage/AP Images, 39; Austin McAfee/AP Images, 41

Cataloging-in-Publication Data
Gitlin, Marty.
Ole Miss Rebels / Marty Gitlin.
   p. cm. -- (Inside college football)
Includes bibliographical references and index.
ISBN 978-1-61783-655-8
1. Ole Miss Rebels (Football team)--History--Juvenile literature. 2. University of Mississippi--Football--History--Juvenile literature. I. Title.
796.332--dc15

2012945809

TABLE OF CONTENTS

Ole Miss quarterback Eli Manning scrambles and searches for a receiver during the 2004 Cotton Bowl.

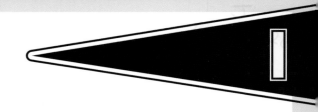

LIKE FATHER, LIKE SON

UNIVERSITY OF MISSISSIPPI QUARTERBACK ELI MANNING WAS NOT JUST COMPETING AGAINST DEFENSIVE BACKS TRYING TO INTERCEPT HIS PASSES. HE WAS NOT ONLY TRYING TO ESCAPE LINEBACKERS SEEKING SACKS. HE WAS FIGHTING AGAINST HIS OWN LAST NAME.

Eli's father, Archie Manning, had been a superstar quarterback at the same school, which is known as Ole Miss. Eli's brother, Peyton Manning, was already one of the greatest quarterbacks in the National Football League (NFL). And critics were telling Eli that he would never be as good as either one of them.

This could have proved challenging. But Eli Manning did not feel pressure to surpass his dad or brother. He yearned only to perform to the best of his ability, which he had largely done so far at Ole Miss. Now in his senior year, Manning just wanted to end his college career with a huge victory.

MANNING V. MANNING

Eli Manning joined the New York Giants shortly after the 2004 NFL Draft. From the start of his professional career, he was compared to his brother, Peyton Manning. Peyton was among the best in league history. When the younger Manning struggled, some complained he would never be as good as his older brother.

But Eli answered his critics on the field. He led the Giants to Super Bowl titles in the 2007 and 2011 seasons. He was praised for his ability to make big plays with the game on the line. Some even began debating if he was a future Hall of Famer after his second Super Bowl title.

"I've never tried to compete with Peyton," Eli said. "I never tried to say I need to be better than him. . . . I'm going to go out and be the best quarterback I can be and get the most out of my potential. If that's better than him, great. If it's not, so be it."

It was January 2, 2004. The Ole Miss Rebels were in Dallas for the Cotton Bowl. They had just wrapped up the regular season with a 9–3 record. That was their best record in more than a decade. Now they looked to beat the Oklahoma State Cowboys in the bowl game. A win would give Ole Miss 10 victories for the first time since the 1971 season.

Approximately 74,000 fans filled the Cotton Bowl stadium. The Rebels opened the scoring in the first quarter. Manning fired a 16-yard touchdown pass to senior running back Tremaine Turner. The Cowboys battled back with two touchdowns to take the lead. But Manning hit sophomore wide receiver Mike Espy for a 25-yard touchdown pass to tie the game before the half.

The drama was just beginning. The Rebels took to the ground in the second half. Turner felt he had something to prove. The Cowboys were known for their strong run game. Their rushing

offense was the twelfth best in the nation. But Turner was the rushing star in the second half. He slashed through the Cowboys' defense, rushing for 45 yards on a third-quarter drive. He capped it with a touchdown burst that gave Ole Miss a 24–14 lead.

Then Manning took over. He threw a 22-yard pass to Espy. He then completed a 20-yard pass to junior wide receiver Kerry Johnson. Manning ran the ball into the end zone to put the Rebels ahead 31–14.

The Cowboys responded with a frantic comeback. They scored two quick touchdowns in the fourth quarter. That cut the Rebels' lead to 31–28. Fewer than five minutes remained in the game. Ole Miss needed to run out the clock. That meant Manning could not use his strong passing arm. The Rebels could not risk the clock stopping after incomplete passes.

The Rebels got to work. Soon it was third down on the Cowboys' 49-yard line. Oklahoma State was out of timeouts. Ole Miss needed just four yards for the first down. That would seal the game. Manning took the snap and handed the ball to Turner. He sprinted for 25 yards.

The clock still ticked. But the game was over. Turner finished with 133 yards on 20 carries—not bad considering he had been sick that week. "I was very motivated coming into this game," he said. "All the talk about how good Oklahoma State was with the run, but we're the ones who got it done."

GOODBYE, COLONEL REB

A tradition died at Ole Miss in 2003. That is when the school retired its mascot. Colonel Reb had been the mascot since 1979. He was a bearded "southern gentleman." But he also embodied the old South. The old South embraced slavery and segregation, which was when blacks were separated from white society. Ole Miss students voted in 2010 to replace the colonel with the Rebel Black Bear. The school also banned Confederate flags at the stadium. The flag represented Southern states during the Civil War. Ole Miss coaches had complained that such symbols made it harder to recruit top black players.

The Rebels had been getting it done since October. Their offense had averaged an incredible 40.5 points in the first four games. Yet they lost two of those games due to the struggling defense. After that, though, the team won seven of its next eight games. And in six of those games, the defense gave up 20 points or fewer.

The only defeat during that stretch was painful. Ole Miss was ranked fifteenth in the nation going into its eleventh game. It faced the third-ranked Louisiana State University (LSU) Tigers at home. A win would have clinched the Southeastern Conference (SEC) West title. A record crowd of 62,552 packed Vaught-Hemingway Stadium for the showdown.

LIKE FATHER, LIKE SON

Ole Miss started the scoring in the first quarter. Sophomore defensive back Travis Johnson returned an interception for a touchdown. However, the Tigers' defense came out strong after that. Manning and the Rebels' powerful offense did not put up a single point until the fourth quarter. Manning's touchdown pass to sophomore running back Brandon Jacobs pulled Ole Miss within three points. The score was 17–14.

Less than 11 minutes remained in the game. Soon Ole Miss got the ball back. Manning began driving his offense down the field. He fired a 31-yard pass to junior receiver Bill Flowers. Turner then rushed for 15 more yards. It appeared that Ole Miss was on its way to victory.

The march stalled short of the end zone. But the Rebels were in field-goal range. Junior kicker Jonathan Nichols just needed to hit from 36 yards to tie the game. It was a kick he usually made easily. But he missed it. It was his second blown field goal of the day.

"Everything was perfect," Nichols said. "I thought I hit it real good. When I looked up, it faded right on me. Man, it's not a good feeling."

NICHOLS WAS USUALLY SOLID

Ole Miss kicker Jonathan Nichols missed the game-tying field goal in the 2003 showdown against LSU. But the Rebels might not have earned a Cotton Bowl spot that year without his efforts. Nichols was named first-team all-SEC. He also earned the Lou Groza Award. It is presented each year to the top kicker in college football. Nichols made 25 of his 29 field goal attempts and all 49 of his extra point attempts that season.

It was not a good feeling for his teammates, either. Manning completed less than half his passes and threw an interception in the defeat. Many believed that game cost him a chance to win the Heisman Trophy. It is awarded each year to the top player in college football.

The loss to LSU did not ruin the Rebels' season, though. Manning still finished third in the voting for the Heisman Trophy. He then led the Rebels to victory in the Cotton Bowl. It capped off a great college career and a great season. Ole Miss fans hoped the season would once again cement the team as one of the nation's best.

LIKE FATHER, LIKE SON

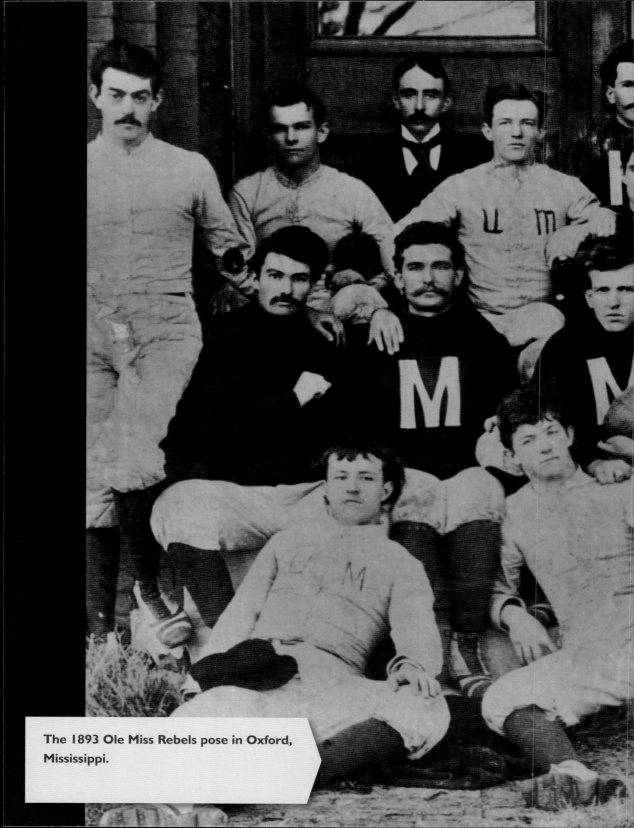

The 1893 Ole Miss Rebels pose in Oxford, Mississippi.

2

FROM BONDURANT TO VAUGHT

THE SOUTHWESTERN BAPTIST UNIVERSITY FOOTBALL PLAYERS COULD HARDLY BELIEVE THEIR EYES. IT WAS NOVEMBER 11, 1893. THEY HAD JUST GOTTEN OFF THE TRAIN IN OXFORD, MISSISSIPPI. FRIENDLY UNIVERSITY OF MISSISSIPPI STUDENTS SURROUNDED THE VISITORS. HORSE-DRAWN CARRIAGES WERE WAITING FOR THEM AS WELL. THE SOUTHERN BAPTIST PLAYERS JOINED THEIR MISSISSIPPI RIVALS ON A RIDE THROUGH TOWN.

The Ole Miss Rebels would not be as nice on the football field that day. It was the first game in school history. And they routed their new rivals 56–0. Ole Miss coach Alexander Lee Bondurant described the scene.

"The afternoon was bright with just enough crispness in the air to inspire vigorous play, and the crowd . . . that surged up University Street . . . showed that this community was prepared to enter with zest into the excitement attendant upon a football game," he said.

"TADPOLE" SMITH

The Rebels have boasted many players with odd nicknames. But none was more colorful than punt returner C. M. "Tadpole" Smith. When Smith was a young boy, he fell into a drainage ditch near a schoolhouse. He was drawn under the road. The ditch was deep and muddy. Smith finally came out. When he did, somebody told him he looked like a tadpole. The nickname stuck.

Smith had blazing speed and quickness. He did not want anything weighing him down. So he refused to wear a helmet. He even taped his ears to his head when he played. Football rules were much more relaxed than they are today. Smith ended his college career in 1928. He returned to the school in 1946 as its athletic director. Smith then directed the greatest sports era in Ole Miss history.

The excitement grew when Ole Miss also shut out its next two opponents. Right from the start, the Rebels began a tradition of great defense. It would soon be their trademark. They blanked 10 of their first 16 opponents. The Rebels had a 13–3 record during that stretch.

However, the school could not find a full-time coach. The instability took a toll. In 1907, Ole Miss lost all six of its games by a combined score of 195–6.

No coach lasted more than two consecutive seasons until 1909. That is when Nathan Stauffer took over. He brought the program back to life by rejuvenating the defense. That defense recorded seven shutouts in eight games in 1910. The only exception was a 9–2 loss at Vanderbilt. It cost Ole Miss the Southern Conference title. Legendary sportswriter Grantland Rice praised the Rebels for their performance.

"The fight proved to be one of the hardest that [Vanderbilt] has seen in many a day," he wrote. "Mississippi

brought the best [team] into the October snowbelt that the Red and Blue has ever finished. . . . Mississippi no longer ranks as a second-class [team]."

The success did not last, though. Stauffer lasted just three seasons. The program slipped into a long period of mediocrity after that. From 1911 to 1934, the best record Ole Miss could muster was 6–3. One of the highlights of that era was in 1933. That year, the Rebels became a charter member of the SEC. They remain a member today.

That 1933 season was also when Ole Miss found its first long-term coach. By 1935, Ed Walker had turned the Rebels into winners. They finished that year 9–3 and recorded six shutouts. However, Ole Miss lost to Catholic University in the Orange Bowl. Nevertheless, it marked the school's first bowl game appearance.

The teams of that era featured the first star players in Ole Miss history. The best were offensive tackle Frank "Bruiser" Kinard and running backs Ray Hapes and Rab Rodgers. Kinard is still considered by some as one of the greatest tackles in college football history. Hapes was known for his exciting style and ability to score touchdowns. And Rodgers was so elusive that he was nicknamed the "Tupelo Ghost."

Another star running back soon followed. He led the team to even greater heights. Parker Hall was named an All-American in 1938. He led the nation in scoring that season with 73 points and an average of 6.5 yards per carry. Harry Mehre had taken over as coach that year. He used Hall as a kick returner and a defensive back, as well. Hall topped the

UP, UP, AND AWAY

In 1937, the Rebels became the first college football team to fly to an away game. At that time, teams took buses or trains to away games. They took an American Airlines plane from Memphis, Tennessee, to Philadelphia, Pennsylvania. There they played at night against Temple University. The legendary Pop Warner coached Temple at the time. He helped create the famous youth football leagues that are named after him. This contest ended in a 0–0 tie.

country in kickoff returns, punt returns, and interception return yards. He was responsible for 22 touchdowns that year.

It is no wonder the Rebels steamrolled to a 9–2 record in 1938. The first of those victories was the most important. It came in the season opener against LSU. The Tigers had not lost to the Rebels in 11 years. Many favored LSU to win easily. But Mehre believed half the battle was convincing his players they could win.

"Men, there's no reason why Ole Miss can't beat anybody," he told them. "What does LSU have over you? They don't have anything over you that hard work and dedication can't overcome."

Mehre was right. Hall stunned the Tigers with a touchdown pass to Ham Murphy. Ole Miss was on its way to a 20–7 victory. It marked the first of four consecutive wins over LSU.

Meanwhile, Mehre emerged as one of the most successful coaches in Ole Miss history. His teams had a combined 25–6 record in his first three seasons. But events far from home were taking a toll on every

college football program in the United States. The Japanese bombed
Pearl Harbor in Hawaii on December 7, 1941. It resulted in thousands
of young US men heading overseas to fight in World War II. That
included football players. With so many players missing, the Ole Miss
football team struggled from 1942 to 1946. The war ended in 1945. In
1947, new coach Johnny Vaught took over. The greatest era in Ole Miss
football history was about to begin.

FROM BONDURANT TO VAUGHT

Ole Miss coach Johnny Vaught poses at the Rebels' home stadium in 1951.

3

THE ERA OF GREATNESS

T WAS EARLY JANUARY 1947. THE REBELS HAD JUST COMPLETED A TERRIBLE SEASON. THEY HAD FALLEN ON HARD TIMES SINCE THE END OF WORLD WAR II IN 1945. AND THEY OWNED AN 8–18 RECORD OVER THE PAST THREE YEARS.

The program was in disarray. Coach Harold "Red" Drew had left for the University of Alabama after just one season at Ole Miss. He recommended backfield coach Tilden Campbell as his replacement. But athletic director Tad Smith had no intention of following that advice. He instead promoted line coach Johnny Vaught.

It was the most fateful decision in Ole Miss football history. Vaught proved to be one of college football's greatest innovators. He introduced new formations and shifts. They maximized the potential of his offensive players and confused defenses. Vaught also prepared tirelessly to create game plans best suited to stop each opponent.

REBELS

FROM REBEL TO GIANT

Before Archie Manning arrived, the finest quarterback in Ole Miss history was Charlie Conerly. And like the two great Mannings of later generations, Conerly blossomed into an NFL star.

It was a long road to get there. Conerly came to Ole Miss in 1942 but missed three years while serving in the Marine Corps in World War II. After strong 1946 and 1947 seasons at Ole Miss, he joined the NFL's New York Giants in 1948. Conerly remained the Giants' starter until 1961.

Conerly finished his NFL career with 19,488 passing yards and 173 touchdowns. He turned the Giants into a perennial title contender. He led them to a 58–31–1 record and five playoff berths in 14 seasons. And in 1956, Conerly led his team to the NFL championship. The Super Bowl did not yet exist. Conerly was voted into the Pro Bowl that season and also in 1950.

In addition, Vaught recruited fine talent. He inherited some great players, too. Quarterback Charlie Conerly was one of them. Conerly combined to pass and rush for 1,784 yards in 1947. He also threw for 18 touchdowns. The result was a 9–2 record, Ole Miss' first SEC title, and a Delta Bowl win.

The Rebels followed with an 8–1 mark in 1948. But the success was short-lived. They wallowed in mediocrity the next three years.

The era of greatness truly began on November 15, 1952. That was the day the Maryland Terrapins came to Oxford riding a 22-game winning streak. They were expected to leave with a 23-game winning streak.

Instead, they left with a stinging defeat. Ole Miss quarterback Jimmy Lear completed 11 of his 16 passes for 231 yards. He added 50 rushing yards. Lear fired a 42-yard pass to split end James Slay to set up the winning touchdown.

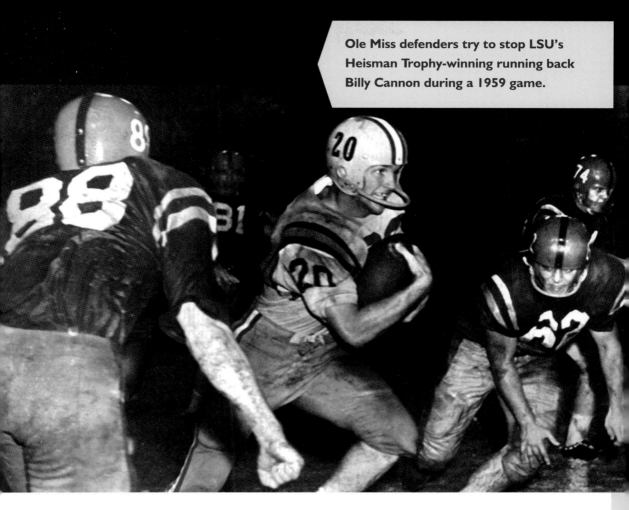

The Associated Press chose the 21–14 victory as the biggest sports upset of the year. *Jackson Daily News* sportswriter Carl Walters called it the "most significant victory ever recorded by a Mississippi football team."

There would soon be many more memorable victories. The Rebels blossomed into a national power. They earned another SEC crown in 1954. The defense gave up just 4.7 points per game during the regular season. Then the Rebels cruised to a 10–1 record in 1955. They capped that season with a 14–13 victory over Texas Christian University in the

Cotton Bowl. It marked the first major bowl win in school history. The best was still yet to come, though.

The Rebels began to peak in 1959. They gave up just 21 points in 10 regular-season games. However, seven of those came in a loss to LSU. It was the Rebels' lone loss that season. But they had an opportunity for revenge when they again met LSU in the Sugar Bowl. And this time, a win would give the Rebels the national title.

Before more than 81,000 fans, the Rebels achieved both. The showdown was scoreless until late in the first half. Then Ole Miss quarterback Jake Gibbs tossed a 43-yard touchdown pass to running back Cowboy Woodruff.

That ended up being all the Rebels needed. Their defense never allowed the Tigers past the Ole Miss 34-yard-line. They held LSU to minus-15 rushing yards for the game. Rebels backup quarterback Bobby Franklin fired two more touchdown passes in the second half as his team won 21–0.

ONE GREAT GUARD

Only two Ole Miss players ever earned a spot in the Pro Football Hall of Fame through 2012. One was Frank "Bruiser" Kinard. He played in the early days of pro football, from 1938 to 1947. The other was Gene Hickerson. Hickerson played guard for the Rebels in the late 1950s. He then became a mainstay for the powerful Cleveland Browns in the late 1950s and 1960s. He blocked for the legendary Jim Brown. Many consider Brown to be the greatest running back in football history.

The Rebels took their momentum and ran with it into the 1960 season. The combination of Gibbs and senior wide receiver Bobby Crespino led the offense. The defense gave up an average of just 6.4 points per game. Ole Miss finished the regular season 9–0–1 and was invited back to the Sugar Bowl. There it defeated Rice 14–6 for its second straight national title.

Ole Miss was in the news in the fall of 1962. But the focus was on the university, not on the football team. The school refused to admit a black student named James Meredith that year. The South was segregated at the time. That meant blacks and whites could legally be separated. Ole Miss was one of many schools that was closed to blacks.

Mississippi Governor Ross Barnett attended the first home game of that season. He made a speech at halftime on the 50-yard line. The federal government had ordered the school to admit Meredith. Barnett sought support from the students to defy that order.

Fighting broke out on campus the next day. Students rioted against officials who were seeking to ensure that Meredith was admitted. Rebels fullback Buck Randall begged the students to go home. "If you don't leave, they're going to start shooting," he said.

His pleas were ignored. Soon 20,000 army troops arrived. Two people were killed and 300 others were injured. Coach Vaught called his players together. He told them their job was to play football and show the American people that they were not like those rioting.

The Rebels delivered. Their 13–6 win over archrival Mississippi State completed a 9–0 regular season. It was the school's first season without a loss or a tie. All-American defensive lineman Jim Dunaway led the way. The defense gave up an average of just 4.4 points in those nine games.

BATTLE FOR THE GOLDEN EGG

The annual showdown between Ole Miss and Mississippi State is known as the Egg Bowl. The winner earns a trophy called the Golden Egg. The in-state rivals had been playing every season since 1901. But the Golden Egg was not awarded until 1927. The idea of the Golden Egg was hatched after a fight broke out between fans following a 1926 Rebels victory over Mississippi State. Students from both schools used the trophy to soothe tensions between the fans of the two teams.

The Rebels returned to the Sugar Bowl. They just needed a win over Arkansas to claim a likely national championship. Ole Miss rose to the occasion. Senior quarterback Glynn Griffing was the star. He fired a 33-yard touchdown pass to senior wingback Louis Guy. He later scored on a 1-yard run to give his team a 17–13 victory and the national title.

"When Ole Miss needed to survive and build a new image, as it sorely did in 1962, a great football team stepped forward," Vaught wrote. "I will always rate the 1962 team as one of the most courageous in the history of the game."

The Rebels won their sixth SEC title in 10 years the following season. But their run of excellence was ending. An era of average football was about to begin.

THE ERA OF GREATNESS

Ole Miss quarterback Archie Manning throws a pass during a 1969 game against Tennessee.

4

A DROUGHT IN MISSISSIPPI

THE REBELS ENJOYED SOME FINE SEASONS FROM THE MID-1960s INTO THE NEW MILLENNIUM. THEIR TEAMS FEATURED MANY GREAT PLAYERS. BUT THEY LOST AT LEAST THREE GAMES EVERY SEASON EXCEPT FOR ONE. AND THEY DID NOT CAPTURE ANY SEC CHAMPIONSHIPS.

The Johnny Vaught era continued through 1970. He produced one winning season after another. But the days of playing for national championships were over. Other SEC programs, such as Alabama, Georgia, and Florida, were becoming stronger. They made it tougher to win league titles.

The Rebels opened the 1964 season as the top-ranked team in the country. But they finished with a disappointing 5–5–1 record. Vaught spent much of the 1960s searching for a quarterback who could move well. The college game was changing. Quarterbacks who could throw on the run had become valuable.

In 1968, Vaught found his new quarterback. He was a redhead from the Mississippi town of Drew. His name was Archie Manning. Manning shattered 27 school records and four SEC records in 1969 alone. He completed 58 percent of his passes that season. That was good for 1,762 yards and nine touchdowns. He also ran for 502 yards and 14 touchdowns.

Manning could not transform the Rebels into SEC champions. But he did guide them to winning records. As a junior in 1969, he led them to a Sugar Bowl win over Arkansas.

Manning's last college season marked the end of Vaught's career as the coach at Ole Miss. The 61-year-old coach had been leading the Rebels for 24 seasons. He did not intend to leave his post. But a doctor told Vaught that the pressure of being a head coach could kill him. He had no choice but to step down.

New coach Billy Kinard got off to a strong start at Ole Miss. He led the 1971 Rebels to a 10–2 record. Ole Miss beat Georgia Tech in that year's Peach Bowl.

Kinard also recruited a number of talented players. Included was star defensive tackle Ben Williams. He became the first black player to wear a Rebels uniform. Williams played at Ole Miss until 1975. He had 377 tackles during that time. He also set a Rebels record by recording 17 sacks in 1973. Williams was voted a first-team All-American in 1975.

Kinard had been fired midway through the 1973 season. Ole Miss fans were excited when Vaught returned to coach the rest of the year. But Vaught again retired after that year to become the school's athletic director.

NO SPEEDING

Manning Way runs just south of Vaught-Hemingway Stadium in Oxford. For years, the speed limit on that road was 18 miles per hour. That was because Archie Manning wore jersey No. 18. However, in 2012 the road changed to 10 miles per hour. That was the jersey number his son, Eli Manning, wore at Ole Miss.

A DROUGHT IN MISSISSIPPI

Vaught promoted assistant coach Ken Cooper to take his place. What followed was a lot of losing. Steve Sloan then replaced Cooper in 1978. But the Rebels did not fare much better under him. They recorded a 41–57–1 record during the tenures of Cooper and Sloan. The period proved to be a shock to Ole Miss fans who had grown used to winning.

Billy Brewer replaced Sloan in 1983. He fared a little better. But his early teams simply could not build success. Star defensive end Freddie Joe Nunn led the 1983 team. He helped the Rebels to their first winning season in seven years. But they sported losing marks in 1984 and 1985. Then they rebounded to win eight games in 1986.

Trouble was brewing for Brewer, though. The National Collegiate Athletic Association (NCAA) cited the program for violating recruiting rules. It placed Ole Miss football on a two-year probation. The Rebels maintained talented players, such as All-American tight end Wesley Walls. But they went just 8–14 in those two seasons.

END TO END

Wesley Walls had played three years at defensive end for Ole Miss in the late 1980s. But coaches decided to also play him at tight end in 1988. That certainly worked out well. Walls was an All-American choice at that position for the Rebels. He was then picked in the second round of the 1989 NFL Draft. He later blossomed into one of the best tight ends in the league. Walls finished his NFL career with 450 catches for 5,291 yards and 54 touchdowns. He was voted into the Pro Bowl five times.

Ole Miss tight end Wesley Walls celebrates after a big play during a 1988 game at home against Tulane.

Brewer finally brought back sustained success in the late 1980s and early 1990s. The Rebels recorded a mark of 31–16 during a four-year period. They peaked in 1992. The defense held five opponents to fewer than 10 points that year. And Ole Miss finished with a 9–3 record. It closed out the year with a 13–0 win over Air Force in the Liberty Bowl.

Ole Miss coach Tommy Tuberville raises the Egg Bowl trophy following a 1995 win over Mississippi State.

Unfortunately, those running the program had not learned their lesson. Another NCAA investigation alleged 15 more recruiting violations. The scandal rocked Ole Miss athletics. Athletic director Warner Alford resigned in June 1994. And Brewer was fired three weeks later.

Joe Lee Dunn coached Ole Miss in 1994. Then the school picked Texas A&M defensive coordinator Tommy Tuberville to take over in 1995. He helped the program recover from the punishments handed down by the NCAA. But the team fared no better on the field. The Rebels managed a 25–20 record in his four seasons.

In 1998, Tuberville was asked to address rumors that he was leaving Ole Miss for another coaching job. He replied, "They'll have to carry me out of here in a pine box." Those words soothed the fears of Rebels fans. Four days later, however, Tuberville resigned to take over the coaching job at SEC rival Auburn.

The Ole Miss program was in disarray. It took a new coach and a brilliant new quarterback to put the pieces back together.

CHUCKY MULLINS

Ole Miss hosted Vanderbilt for homecoming on October 28, 1989. Commodores tailback Brad Gaines jumped up to catch a pass. Rebels safety Chucky Mullins lowered his shoulders and tackled him. It was a play made on college football fields across America every Saturday. But this time, Mullins did not get up. He was rushed to the hospital with a shattered neck. Gaines visited him. So did Chicago Bears superstar Walter Payton, singer Janet Jackson, and even President George H. W. Bush.

Mullins was in critical condition. But he had the strength to mumble words that he wanted to say to Gaines. "It wasn't your fault," Mullins whispered.

Gaines was so shaken that he never played his senior season. He gave the eulogy at the funeral after Mullins died from his injuries. And nearly 20 years later, Gaines was still visiting Mullins's grave three times a year.

quarterback Romaro Miller
o pass as a Tulane defender
nim during a 1999 game.

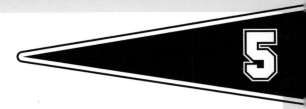

5

NEW REBELS

MOST COACHES ARE HIRED BETWEEN SEASONS. IT GIVES THEM PLENTY OF TIME TO PREPARE FOR THEIR NEW JOBS. BUT DAVID CUTCLIFFE DID NOT HAVE THAT LUXURY.

Cutcliffe was named the Ole Miss coach after Tommy Tuberville bolted for Auburn in December 1998. The Rebels were three weeks away from their biggest game of the season. They were getting ready to play Texas Tech in the Independence Bowl.

Cutcliffe refused to complain, though. He instead spoke about becoming familiar with his players. He knew that would help him in the future. And he knew there was no time to make drastic changes that season anyway.

But there was one huge problem. Cutcliffe spent Christmas in the hospital. He had an inflamed pancreas. The coach was released in time for the game. He coached in pain. But he certainly had his Rebels ready.

Ole Miss sophomore quarterback Romaro Miller played despite having broken his collarbone a month earlier. And he still managed to set an Independence Bowl record with three touchdown passes. One was a 26-yard pass to sophomore wide receiver Cory Peterson with eight minutes left. Ole Miss sophomore defensive back Anthony Magee intercepted a pass 30 seconds later. That sealed the Rebels' 35–18 win.

The Independence Bowl showdown also featured two of the finest running backs in college football. Ricky Williams starred for Texas Tech. But Ole Miss sophomore Deuce McAllister outshined him. McAllister scored three touchdowns. Meanwhile, the Rebels held Williams to 85 yards and no touchdowns.

The future was looking bright for Ole Miss. The Rebels had won with just six seniors on the roster. Cutcliffe knew he had most of his players returning the following season. So he was energized, despite having been in the hospital a week earlier.

STAYING IN THE SOUTH

Running back Deuce McAllister was born and raised in Mississippi. He played for the Rebels. And he did not leave the South when he left for the NFL. The New Orleans Saints selected McAllister in the first round of the 2001 NFL Draft. He became one of the most feared runners in the league. He rushed for more than 3,000 yards combined in 2002 and 2003. He was voted into the Pro Bowl both seasons. However, knee injuries eventually took a toll on his career. He was out of the NFL by 2009.

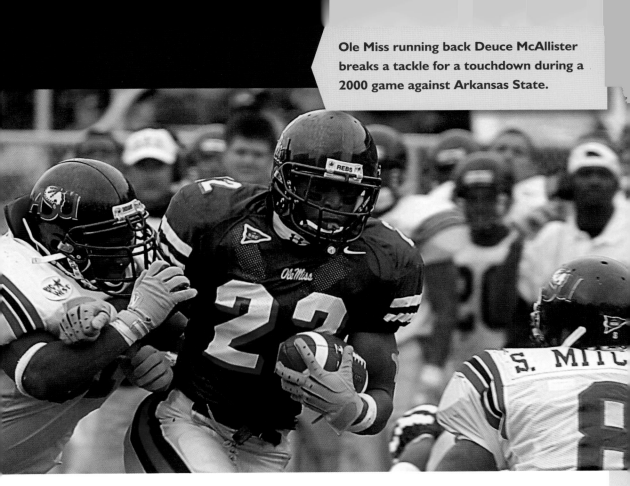

The Rebels finished 7–4 in the 1999 regular season. That earned them another trip to the Independence Bowl. This time they ended the season with a 27–25 win over Oklahoma.

The future once again looked bright for Ole Miss. A new recruit made it look even brighter. Cutcliffe had called high school quarterback Eli Manning soon after taking over as coach. Manning knew all about Cutcliffe. He knew that Cutcliffe had coached his brother Peyton at Tennessee. He knew that Cutcliffe had helped Peyton become a great NFL quarterback. And Manning knew then that he wanted to follow in the footsteps of his father and wear an Ole Miss uniform.

REBELS

PATRICK WILLIS

The battles Patrick Willis faces on the field pale in comparison to those he has overcome in life. The former Ole Miss linebacker's parents separated when he was four. He was forced to work in a cotton field at age 10 to help support his family. His basketball coach became his legal guardian six years later because Willis's father neglected him and abused his younger siblings. His younger brother drowned at age 21.

"My real-life experience has taught me how to compete through adversity, no matter what the situation was," Willis said.

Willis was arguably the greatest linebacker in Rebels history. He recorded an incredible 265 tackles in his last two seasons combined at Ole Miss, in 2005 and 2006. He then exceeded 100 tackles in each of his first four seasons with the NFL's San Francisco 49ers. Willis was named to the Pro Bowl in each of his first five years.

The younger Manning enjoyed a brilliant college career. He helped Ole Miss improve. But he could not help the Rebels win consistently. Other SEC teams had top-end players at every position. Ole Miss simply could not keep up. That was especially true on defense.

Manning left Ole Miss on a high note in 2003. He guided his team to an SEC West title. And he capped the season with the Cotton Bowl victory. But it became apparent that Ole Miss would need more elite players.

That became even clearer after Manning left. Cutcliffe was fired after the Rebels fell to 4–7 in 2004. Four straight losses late in the season sealed his fate. Athletic director Pete Boone said Cutcliffe refused to submit a plan to fix problems within the program. Among them was a defense that usually ranked near the bottom of the SEC.

However, the situation only got worse when University of Southern California assistant coach Ed Orgeron

[38]

replaced Cutcliffe. He set out to recruit top talent to his new school. *The Sporting News* had named him the 2004 Recruiter of the Year.

Nevertheless, the Rebels struggled on the field for three seasons under Orgeron. Their record was 10–25 during that time. But Orgeron lived up to his reputation in recruiting a linebacker named Patrick Willis. He proved to be one of the best in school history. Willis earned first-team All-America and SEC Defensive Player of the Year honors in 2005 and 2006. He also won the 2006 Butkus Award as the premier linebacker in college football.

NEW REBELS

Willis left for the NFL after the 2006 season. Orgeron was fired after the 2007 season. Former Arkansas coach Houston Nutt replaced him. The losing stopped for two seasons under Nutt. He guided the Rebels to back-to-back winning records and Cotton Bowl victories. Brothers Peria Jerry and John Jerry were All-American defensive linemen during that time. Running back Dexter McCluster shined as well. He gained 1,824 rushing yards and 1,145 receiving yards in his junior and senior years combined.

Ole Miss had matching 9–4 records and Cotton Bowl wins in 2008 and 2009. The last time the school had back-to-back nine-plus-win seasons was in 1961 and 1962. Johnny Vaught was still coaching at the time.

McCluster ran wild in an upset victory over Oklahoma State in the Cotton Bowl after the 2009 season. He sprinted for an 86-yard touchdown in the second quarter. In the process, he became the first SEC player to gain 1,000 rushing yards and 500 receiving yards in one

THE BLIND SIDE

Ole Miss offensive tackle Michael Oher was one of the best college players at his position. Offensive linemen often do not get much attention. However, millions of people learned about Oher's life story in the 2009 movie *The Blind Side*. It was based on a book called *The Blind Side: Evolution of a Game*. Oher was a homeless and troubled teenager. Then a caring family took him in and nurtured him. He blossomed as a player and as a person before starring at Ole Miss. Oher earned first-team All-America honors as a senior in 2008. He then went on to play tackle for the Baltimore Ravens of the NFL.

season. McCluster ended that game with 184 rushing yards and two touchdowns. But McCluster left for the NFL after that 2009 season. The Rebels' record dropped to 4–8 the next season. Then, in 2011, they went just 2–10 and 0–8 in the SEC. It was their worst season in 104 years.

When it was over, Nutt was forced to resign. Hugh Freeze replaced him. Freeze had turned Arkansas State into a winner. Turning Ole Miss into a winner would be a bigger task. The Rebels' national titles of the late 1950s and early 1960s were becoming a distant memory. Only time would tell if Freeze could bring the same glory back to Ole Miss football.

TIMELINE

Ole Miss shuts out Southwestern Baptist 56–0 in its first-ever football game on November 11.

The Rebels are outscored 195–6 in the worst season in their history.

Ole Miss wins the first Egg Bowl with a 20–12 victory over Mississippi A&M—later Mississippi State—on November 24.

After three years serving in the Marine Corps during World War II, quarterback Charlie Conerly returns to Ole Miss for the first of two standout seasons.

The SEC champion Rebels defeat Texas Christian 13–9 in the Delta Bowl on January 1 to cap the first year under new coach Johnny Vaught.

1893 1907 1927 1946 1948

Standout quarterback Archie Manning begins his college career at Ole Miss.

Vaught steps down as coach after 24 years due to health concerns and is replaced by Billy Kinard. The Rebels finish 10–2 after a Peach Bowl victory over Georgia Tech.

First-year coach Billy Brewer begins a coaching stint marked by recruiting violations and NCAA punishments.

Brewer is fired as coach in July after more allegations of recruiting violations.

The Rebels defeat Texas Tech 35–18 in the Independence Bowl on December 31. Weeks earlier, David Cutcliffe had taken over as coach for Tommy Tuberville.

1968 1971 1983 1994 1998

Ole Miss breaks Maryland's 22-game winning streak with a 21–14 win on November 15. It places the program on the national map.

1952

The Rebels surrender just 47 points throughout the regular season to win the SEC championship.

1954

A 21–0 victory over LSU in the Sugar Bowl on January 1 gives Ole Miss its first national title.

1960

The Rebels clinch their second national championship with a 14–6 defeat of Rice in the Sugar Bowl on January 2.

1961

Ole Miss earns its third national title in four years with a 17–13 win over Arkansas in the Sugar Bowl on January 1.

1963

Quarterback Eli Manning leads the Rebels to an SEC West title in 2003 and then a 31–28 win over Oklahoma State in the Cotton Bowl on January 2.

2004

Ed Orgeron replaces Cutcliffe as Ole Miss coach but guides the team to three losing seasons.

2005

Rebels senior Patrick Willis wins the Butkus Award as the top linebacker in college football.

2006

The Rebels beat Oklahoma State 21–7 on January 2 for their second straight Cotton Bowl triumph under coach Houston Nutt.

2010

Ole Miss completes a 2–10 season—its worst since 1907.

2011

QUICK STATS

PROGRAM INFO
University of Mississippi "Ole Miss"
   Rebels (1893–)

NATIONAL CHAMPIONSHIPS
1959*, 1960*, 1962*
*Denotes shared titles

OTHER ACHIEVEMENTS
SEC championships: 6
Bowl record: 21–12

KEY PLAYERS
(POSITION[S]; SEASONS WITH TEAM)
Charlie Conerly (QB; 1942, 1946–47)
Jim Dunaway (OL; 1960–62)
Jake Gibbs (QB; 1958–60)
Glynn Griffing (QB; 1960–62)
Parker Hall (HB; 1936–38)
Frank "Bruiser" Kinard (OT; 1935–37)
Kris Mangum (TE; 1994–96)
Archie Manning (QB; 1968–70)
Eli Manning (QB; 2000–03)
Deuce McAllister (RB; 1997–2000)
Freddie Joe Nunn (DE; 1981–84)

Michael Oher (OT; 2005–08)
Wesley Walls (DE/TE; 1985–88)
Ben Williams (DT; 1972–75)
Patrick Willis (LB; 2003–06)

KEY COACHES
David Cutcliffe (1998–2004)
   44–29; 4–1 (bowl games)
Harry Mehre (1938–42; 1944–45)
   39–26–1
Johnny Vaught (1947–70)
   190–61–12; 11–8 (bowl games)

HOME STADIUM
Vaught-Hemingway Stadium (1915–)

* All statistics through 2011 season

The first Ole Miss coach, Alexander Lee Bondurant, used an actual pig bladder as the first football of his childhood. He would kick it around with his friends near his Virginia home. When he held his first football practice at Ole Miss, he learned that many of his players also had played with a pig bladder on their farms as kids.

"Manning is so elusive and so dangerous running that he breaks down any pass defense. He motors backwards, sideward, and upward. When you close in on him, he finds someone open. . . . Manning has to go down as the best quarterback I have seen in the SEC." —Harry Mehre, former Rebels coach and football analyst for the *Atlanta Journal*, on Ole Miss quarterback Archie Manning

Rebels star quarterback Charlie Conerly later played in arguably the most famous game in NFL history. His touchdown pass gave the New York Giants a 17–14 lead over the Baltimore Colts in the 1958 NFL Championship Game. But the Colts came back to win in overtime on national television. The historic game has been credited with popularizing the NFL.

GLOSSARY

All-American
A player chosen as one of the best amateurs in the country in a particular activity.

archrival
A team's most disliked opponent.

athletic director
An administrator who oversees the coaches, players, and teams of an institution.

charter member
An original; involved since the beginning.

conference
In sports, a group of teams that play each other each season.

draft
A system used by professional sports leagues to select new players in order to spread incoming talent among all teams. The NFL Draft is held each spring.

mediocrity
Not bad but not good.

probation
A period of time where a person or team tries to make up for wrongdoing.

recruiting
Trying to entice a player to come to a certain school. The players being enticed are called recruits.

resign
To quit a job or position.

segregated
When two groups of people are legally kept apart.

upset
A game in which the team expected to lose ends up winning.

FOR MORE INFORMATION

FURTHER READING

Boyles, Bob, and Paul Guido. *The USA Today College Football Encyclopedia*. New York, NY: Skyhorse Publishing, 2011.

Scott, Richard. *SEC Football: 75 Years of Pride and Passion*. Minneapolis, MN: MVP Books, 2008.

WEB LINKS

To learn more about the Ole Miss Rebels, visit ABDO Publishing Company online at **www.abdopublishing.com**. Web sites about the Rebels are featured on our Book Links page. These links are routinely monitored and updated to provide the most current information available.

PLACES TO VISIT

College Football Hall of Fame
111 South St. Joseph St.
South Bend, IN 46601
1-800-440-FAME (3263)
www.collegefootball.org

This hall of fame and museum highlights the greatest players and moments in the history of college football. Among the former Rebels enshrined here are Charlie Conerly, Archie Manning, and Frank "Bruiser" Kinard.

Vaught-Hemingway Stadium
All-American & Hill Drive
Oxford, MS 38677
1-662-915-7167
www.olemisssports.com/facilities/ole-facilities-hemingway.html

The Ole Miss Rebels have been playing their home games at this stadium since 1915. Archie Manning played quarterback for the Rebels here, as did his son, Eli. Greats Frank "Bruiser" Kinard and Patrick Willis also played here approximately 80 years apart.

INDEX

ABOUT THE AUTHOR

Marty Gitlin is a freelance writer based in Cleveland, Ohio. He has written more than 60 educational books. Gitlin has won more than 45 awards during his 30 years as a writer, including first place for general excellence from the Associated Press. He lives with his wife and three children.